The IRS Is <u>NOT</u> The 'Big Bad Wolf'

Tax Preparers Are the Ones Who Give the Industry a Bad Name

By:
Germayne Farrell

Table of Contents

"If we can't get you no money – it can't be got"

Dedication

I would like to dedicate this book to our clients that continue to support Farrell Tax and Services. As we grow, we will continue to give you the level of service you need and deserve.

If you are new to us, may you feel as much "at home" as the rest of our loyal clients.

"If we can't get you no money – it can't be got"

Chapter 1

Protecting YOU From
The "Big Bad Wolves"

The book you're holding in your hands can save you lots of money. It will also help you avoid considerable hardships.

Several years ago when I opened my tax office, I never thought I'd be writing a book about it. However, after helping hundreds of people with their taxes, I've noticed an alarming trend that I thought should be shared with the people in the United States. I hope you will see this book as a public service announcement. My partner and I wanted to accomplish two primary goals.

1.) We wanted to give you a general overview of the tax process. That way, when you come in to see us, you'll have a good understanding how things work, and what we will do for you.
2.) We want to make sure you are aware of a few unethical things that occur in the tax community when it comes to getting your taxes prepared.
You should be aware of a few things. For starters, there's a big myth about the tax process that I want to clear up. I also want to warn you about some of the impending

"If we can't get you no money – it can't be got"

dangers you may be confronted with.

The biggest myth is that many people feel like the IRS is the "Big Bad Wolf." That's simply not true.

The real "bad boys "are the tax preparers. They are the ones doing the damage that cause so much misery at tax season. It's the tax preparers who are the "wolves in sheep's clothing." <u>They are the ones you need to be careful dealing with</u>.

The IRS is there to help you. They simply need to have accurate information so the numbers on your taxes add up.

Some people have asked why I would go through all the trouble and expense to share this information with you. The answer is simple. In my opinion, living your life with purpose means doing the right thing. In this case, "doing the right thing" means spreading the word to the tax community so nobody can take advantage of you.

Preparing your taxes should be a simple process. Unfortunately, many people think when it comes to taxes, it's something they should be worried or afraid of. The thought of dealing with the IRS makes many people uncomfortable. They approach the tax process thinking they're going to owe the government money. In most cases that's not true.

The public becomes all worked up over the tax process. The idea of getting their taxes done builds up over several weeks. For some, their anxiety comes from past

"If we can't get you no money – it can't be got"

experiences, because they've had a negative experience. Others have had their taxes done by tax preparers who didn't have a clue what they were doing, and the customer ends up getting audited and owing money to the IRS. You can't really blame anyone for feeling that way. They're simply basing their feelings on negative past experiences.

Some people are afraid to ask questions when they get their taxes done, fearing they'll look unwise. Others have the opinion that the government is out to "get them." It's been my experience as a tax preparer that the IRS is quite easy to work with. The IRS is not out to get you. No one is in their office, determined to catch you doing something wrong. Nothing could be further from the truth.

As tax season rolls around, many people want to sweep their taxes under the carpet, hoping the entire situation will just disappear. Some people get so upset they don't file their taxes. <u>You don't *ever* want to do that</u>.

Always file your taxes. Failure to do so will cause you huge additional problems.

"If we can't get you no money – it can't be got"

Chapter 2

Why Should
Farrell Tax and Services
Prepare My Taxes?

During my years as a tax preparer, I've noticed most people will make their buying decisions much the same way. What I mean by that is it comes down to who we trust. This is especially true when it comes to our taxes and personal finances.

When I'm considering someone to assist me with my personal finances, I should be able to develop a trust towards them.

Many people base their decisions on a referral from someone they trust, like a friend or family member. It's reassuring when someone you trust recommends someone to you.

When one of our clients refers a friend to us, it's almost like we're working for two people; the person that happens to be the new client and the referring individual. Referrals are a huge part of our business. We do everything we can to make them happy and want them to return.

My partner and I could easily grow our business by

"If we can't get you no money – it can't be got"

referrals only. However, that would mean leaving out thousands of people in our community who would end up having to fend for themselves. I wouldn't want that to happen to anyone. Nobody should have to "roll the dice" and wonder if they're dealing with a reputable tax preparer. This book will help people avoid those problems so they can make an informed decision.

I thought the best way to get the word out to our community was to write a book. And while this book could easily have been 500 pages — and that's probably not what you want. If you're like most of our clients, you just want to know the basics about the tax process, and the reassurance that you're dealing with a company that will treat you right.

I've read tax books that an attorney would find difficult to comprehend. Even as a tax professional, I have found some difficult to understand. I doubt that is what you want.

A better option is to have a book that you can pick up and within a few hours have a better understanding of the tax process. That's what we've done with this book; it's friendly, engaging and written in plain English.

"If we can't get you no money – it can't be got"

How We Work
With Our Clients

Our services are very affordable, much less than our competitors. We never ask for money in advance. Our business does not operate in such manner. We'll be clear with you, and explain everything up front. Our message simply states… "If you don't get a tax return, we don't get paid."

We're open year-round. Most tax offices are only open during tax season. I've never understood that. People have tax issues all year long. I mean, what's someone supposed to do if they have a tax issue in the middle of the year and their tax office is closed? Imagine showing up at your tax preparer's office only to find a padlock on the door. As awful as that sounds, it happens all the time!

Many tax preparers run their businesses a lot like Christmas tree lots you see during the holidays. They're eager to take their customer's money during the height of tax season. But the moment tax season is over, many tax offices are nowhere to be found. They leave their clients high and dry. That's no way for a business to treat loyal customers who trusts a company with their information.

You won't have to worry about that with us. We are here every day of the year except New Year's Day, Christmas, and when the banks are closed. We also stand behind our

"If we can't get you no money – it can't be got"

work.

In the unlikely event, you get audited by the IRS, most tax preparers have a program where you can spend $49 and they will work with you in case you are audited. Contrarily it only includes up to a certain number of hours. After that, you're on your own.

We do not operate in this manner. If you are happened to get audited, we stand behind our work. We'll be there for you, and communicate to the IRS on your behalf, beginning to end. We won't charge you anything either. Not one penny.

People come to us all the time from other tax preparers. Many have been audited. When this happens, we walk the client through their audit. Since we stay open all year round, we're going to make sure things get handled for you.

Our fees are more nominal than what most tax preparers charge.

We are very experienced. Between my partner and me, we have more than 40 years of experience. I doubt there are any other tax preparers in our area with our level of experience. Nor do I believe they research in the manner that we do for our clients. Our motto sums it up. "…If we can't get you no money, it can't be got." In other words, if we can't get you a refund, I don't care where you go, it isn't likely to happen.

"If we can't get you no money – it can't be got"

Our clients appreciate that we share everything with them and have full transparency. They like that because many clients have told us they've gone to other tax offices, and often the preparer will purposely keep the computer turned away from them. It's as if the tax preparer was preventing their client from seeing what they're doing. That doesn't add up to me. It would raise an immediate red flag. I can't think of a reason a tax preparer would want to prevent you from seeing what they're doing.

Why would a tax preparer purposely keep their computer turned away from their client? To me, it means they are trying to hide something and they don't want you to see what they're doing. They may be filling in boxes as the software directs them through the tax process. If that's all they're doing, they're not doing their job. Anybody could buy one of those tax software programs, and do their own taxes at home. That's not why you hired a tax preparer.

In my opinion, if someone pays a tax preparer for their professional services, the least they could do was a little research to save their client some money.

The big tax offices are notorious for doing this. They tend to rush their customers through the tax process. Many treat it like an assembly line. They hurry their clients through the process as fast as they can. Time is money. In their eyes the more customers they see, the more money made. Good for them, bad for you.

"If we can't get you no money – it can't be got"

We don't do business that way. We're the opposite. We're very transparent. When you sit down with my partner and me, we want you to see everything we're doing. We'll make it a point to walk you through every phase of the tax process. We take the time to explain what we're doing and why we're doing it. We encourage you to ask questions. We never work with our computer screens turned away from you.

We have a system in our office most tax preparers don't use. I've never been inside another tax office, but this is what I've been told by previous clients.

You don't have to make an appointment. You're welcome to walk in.

Our receptionist will greet you when you walk into our office. She'll take your name and ask you to complete an interview package. You'll then sit down with my partner, Chip Bell.

Chip will ask you a few questions about your taxes and your filing status.

When you're finished talking with Chip, you'll come in and meet with me. I'll review your application with you and ask you a few additional questions. The process will give me a better understanding of your situation. We have many checks and balances in place, which is why we ask so many questions. Unlike most tax preparers, when you work with us, you will have two experienced tax

professionals going over your application, not just one.
Our services are personalized. We understand getting your
taxes done is not something you do every day. The process
makes a lot of people nervous. That's to be expected. We
do our best to understand what you're going through.
We'll do all we can to make you feel comfortable.

We will explain everything to you. We'll also tell you why
we're doing the things we do.

During tax season, most tax preparers try to get as many
clients as they can, as fast as they can.

You see, tax season is short offering only a few months
and because of the shortened season, many "unreliable"
tax offices are only open during this time purposefully.
Their goal is straightforward. They want to make as much
money as they can, in the shortest amount of time possible.

Many tax offices will go to extremes to make that happen,
even if that means saying things that aren't true. They'll
print up flyers promoting huge credits hoping to attract
unsuspecting clients. They don't always tell their clients
the "whole story."

Potential clients go into some tax offices thinking they're
going to get a big tax credit… only to find out that didn't
happen. Many unethical tax offices promise their clients
"the moon," but can't deliver on their promises. For
example, they'll print flyers and say something like…
"We'll get you this, and we'll get you that." The truth is,

"If we can't get you no money – it can't be got"

they only tell half the story. They don't tell clients that the "full Earned Income Tax Credits" are based on an individual's income for the entire year.

Many tax offices are masterful at misleading their clients. They know if they can get a few unsuspecting clients in the door, there's a good chance they'll close some of them, even if that means doing a little "bait and switch" along the way. They know that once a client is in their office — there's a good chance a few won't leave — even if it means getting bad news. It works too. Many clients stay. They say to themselves, "Oh well, Since I am here I might as well stay and deal with my tax filing issues."

It bothers me that so many tax preparers mislead the public. It gives the industry a bad name. A handful of questionable tax offices make it difficult for those who run our businesses ethically. It makes our jobs more difficult.

It is never easy to tell a client a tax preparer misled them. We must advise many people who don't qualify for the tax credit another tax preparer told them they could get.

We must work hard to overcome the "wolves" which are the tax preparers making a substantial living preying on unsuspecting clients. I'll talk more about this in a later chapter. For now, I want you to be aware who you take your taxes to and continue to keep your guard up. On the outside, a tax preparer can appear honest, friendly, and ethical. However, on the inside, they're unethical and out to make money at your expense, without you knowing it's

"If we can't get you no money – it can't be got"

happening. I call these slippery people, "wolves in sheep clothing." Hence, tax preparers in a business suit.

Sadly, we spend a lot of time fixing problems created by other bad tax preparers. It's never easy giving bad news to good people. People that have a little up front awareness could have avoided being taken advantage of by an unethical tax preparer.

Chapter 3

How We Got in The Tax Business

We all have crossroads in our lives. For me, one of those moments occurred several years ago. At the time, I was in the construction business. Business was slowing because of the downturn in the housing market. Around that same time, I began to hear about a tax company in California. They called themselves an "all in one" tax and insurance company. I reached out to them a few times, but never heard from anyone. After a while, I decided to move on.

Not long after, I was introduced to a woman who became my tax accountant. During a meeting together, I told her I was looking for a new profession. She gave me a brochure about a company she thought might be able to help me. The company name was Federal Direct.

Federal Direct offered "startup" partnerships for people who wanted a career in the tax business. I decided to give them a call. They said they were an ideal fit for anyone looking to get started in the tax business. The arrangement was, I'd pay them a one-time upfront fee. I'd be responsible for finding new clients who needed their taxes done. In exchange, Federal Direct would take care of all

"If we can't get you no money – it can't be got"

my back-office accounting needs. It seemed like a good opportunity given my situation.

I decided to move forward with Federal Direct. There was just one problem. I didn't have enough money for the down payment they required. I offered to pay half of the money upfront, and the balance once I acquired a few clients. They agreed.

My timing was perfect. Since it would be several months before tax season started, I had time to get familiar with all the IRS rules and procedures. Federal Direct did exactly what they said they'd do. They provided me with excellent support. At one point, even the V.P. of the company called me personally, to make sure I was doing okay. He wanted to make sure I had a good handle on everything. We ended up developing a nice business relationship.

Things were really looking up. That very same year, Farrell Tax and Services received an award from Federal Direct, voting us "the fastest growing tax office in 2011."

The following year, Federal Direct invited me to an IRS convention. While I was there, I met Federal Direct's owner and vice president at that time. At one point, they were kind enough to fly my sales representative to Florida so she could meet me.

After two years of working with Federal Direct, I decided it was time to part ways.

"If we can't get you no money – it can't be got"

Farrell Tax Services were now 100% free of all ties with Federal Direct. We have been located at 847 Orange Avenue, Suite A1, Daytona Beach, FL 32114, ever since.

After my first year, I received a call from an IRS representative. She asked me to come down to her local office. When I arrived, she told me I was being audited. She warned me and stated, if I didn't get my act together, not only would they shut me down; they'd have me locked up!

As you might imagine, her comments had my full attention. I looked her in the eyes and said, "Thank you for this warning. I told her I would be more careful of such mistakes. Her warning me and the comments she made was the best advice I'd ever received.

I think everybody should have a basic understanding of taxes and how the process works. If you decide not to hire us, at least you are prepared to ask important questions to a potential tax preparer.

Becoming a tax professional was one of the greatest joys of my life. And while I loved what I was doing, I learned a few hard lessons along the way.

My partner, Alvin "Chip" Bell also has an interesting beginning to the tax business. He went to school at Daytona State. Back in 1978, Chip's aunt was routinely doing his taxes. One year, the IRS accidentally shred his taxes. They sent him a letter telling him he would have to

"If we can't get you no money – it can't be got"

complete them again.

He tried to get his aunt to do them, but she was not available. He had no choice but to do his taxes himself. He did some research and completed his own taxes. He's been doing taxes ever since. He started doing taxes for his family and friends, and from that point his business grew.

How Our Paths Crossed

One day, I heard about a guy in the Daytona Beach area who others said was very good at doing taxes. I decided to reach out to him to see if he'd be interested in starting a partnership together. He said, "Let me think about it." But, that wasn't the end of the story.

A few weeks later, I was sitting behind my desk when the same gentleman walked in my office. He stood in the doorway and said, "Germayne, I've decided to accept your offer to be your partner. Are you ready to get to work?" His words were music to my ears. I was ready.

His arrival to Farrell Tax and Services was perfect timing. Alvin "Chip" Bell was officially my new business partner.

Since we have become business partners we have never looked back.

"If we can't get you no money – it can't be got"

Chapter 4

Why I Wrote
This Book

Since Farrell Tax and Services opened, I've heard many horror stories from clients who've been taken advantage of by masquerading so called "professional" tax preparers. These people are anything but professionals. They hand out flyers, promising consumers huge refunds. When people respond to the ads, they end up getting far less than promised and end up being audited by the IRS.

Many of these people will return to their original tax preparer, only to find out the company is closed, or out of business.

That's no way to treat a client and quite frankly, it's unethical.

One of the reasons I decided to write this book is because I wanted the public to know what really occurs in the world of tax preparation. Unlike what most people think, the IRS is not "The Big Bad Wolf." The people you should be careful of are the tax preparers. They're the ones who create the biggest problems for taxpayers.

"If we can't get you no money – it can't be got"

I want clients to know that the IRS is not the problem. The IRS is on your side. They're just doing their job. They're not trying to catch you doing something wrong, as most people think. For the most part, the IRS is there to fix problems created by "bad" tax preparers. The tax preparers are the ones who give the industry "a bad rap." They're the ones who constantly mislead clients.

Until recently, I haven't had an effective method to spread word to the public. Then one day, it hit me and I decide to write a book; so that we could warn people about "so-called" professional tax preparers, who make a living preying on the public. No longer would I have to sit on the sidelines and watch innocent people be taken advantage of year after year.

If this book helps one person from being ripped off by an unethical tax preparer, then I feel I've done my part and it would all be worth it.

"If we can't get you no money – it can't be got"

Chapter 5

Top Questions
You Should Ask
A Tax Preparer

Question #1:

The first thing I recommend you to do is ask the person you're considering doing your taxes is do they have a "PTIN number?"

A "PTIN" is a personal tax identity number that tells the IRS who prepared your tax return. If the person says, "What's a PTIN...?"

That's a good indication the person you're talking to is not qualified to do your taxes, at this moment it is time to pack your things and head for the door.

Question #2:

What are the four ways I can receive my tax return? If a tax preparer tells you the only way you can receive your return is via a check or debit card -- that's incorrect. This is another good indicator that the person you're talking to is not "at the top of their game" as a tax preparer.

"If we can't get you no money – it can't be got"

You Can Receive Your
Tax Return 4 Ways:

1.) A check can be sent directly to you from The United States Treasury Department via the IRS.

2.) You can have your refund check deposited directly into your checking or savings account.

3.) You can receive your tax return via a debit card, issued by the bank the tax company works with. This process is done by issuing you a temporary debit bankcard.

4.) You can get a check electronically printed from the tax office which is issued from one out of the three recognized major IRS banks. These checks will have three parts. One part you sign and the tax preparer's keeps as a record. This indicates you picked up the check from their office. As far as the other two parts… one is the actual check and the other is the receipt.

Questions #3:

How long have you been at your current location?

A legitimate tax office will typically stay at the same location many years. It's not unusual for a tax office to stay at the same location 10, 15, 20 years. This is true unless the company has experienced rapid growth and needs a bigger office. It's a red flag if you see a tax office

"If we can't get you no money – it can't be got"

change addresses every year.

Every tax season, tax preparers come out of the woodwork. For example, in 2011, when we opened our current office, there were only two tax offices on our street. That quickly changed. As the word got out, clients figured that Orange Avenue was the "go to" place to get their taxes done. New tax offices apparently felt the same way. They figured if they opened their doors near us, they would increase their chances of more "walk-in" traffic. As a result, by 2012, there were five tax offices on our street!

Our clients have become accustomed to seeing our office on Orange Avenue. Over the years, Farrell Tax and Services has become an important part of the local landscape.

We're a 3-person office, and during tax season we could possibly serve more than 500 clients. Throughout the year, we help many clients and the number continually increases every year.

Question #4:

Will my tax return come from the IRS or a personal bank account?

Tax preparers are required to file taxes through the IRS Efile system. To use the IRS Efile system you must have "EFIN" number. An EFIN is an electronically file identification number that tells the IRS from what tax office your return originated from. Therefore, to file a return the tax office must utilize several tax offices software available. Your check should never come from an individual's bank account.

Question #5*:*

Are tax preparers held by certain integrity standards?

Many so-called "tax service companies" open during the peak of tax season much like Christmas tree lots during the holidays. But, as soon as tax season is over, many of these unreliable tax offices close their doors.

Some tax companies are extremely bold. For example, we've had clients walk in the wrong tax office thinking they're in our office. When they ask for me or my partner by name, the individual in the office will tell the client we are at lunch, then offer to help them on our behalf. Can you believe someone would do that?

Think about that for a moment. Knowing that some tax preparers are willing to outright lie to a client… what do you think the chances you'd have of being treated honestly and ethically? In my humble opinion, I'd say slim to none.

I've seen clients around town on a day to day basis. They will mention they were in our office recently getting their taxes prepared. I'll ask, "What day were they in?" and they would reply, "A couple of days ago." They'll tell

"If we can't get you no money – it can't be got"

me that they would ask for us by name and were told, we were at lunch, but we can help you."

I'll know immediately that this is false information given to the client because during busy tax season; we never go to lunch. Our offices hours are from 9am to 7pm. No exceptions!

Unfortunately, this kind of activity has been going on for a long time. These are the people who give our industry a bad name. They are the real "wolves dressed in sheep's clothing." We deal with tax preparers like this every tax season. I think it's important you know this. I believe you should know just how widespread it is and understand how unethical some tax preparers can be.

The Dreaded
Tax Audit

I don't know anyone who likes to hear the words, "You're being audited." This is particularly true when it involves their federal tax return.

Throughout the year, we have clients and potential clients visit our office, frantic because they've received a CP2000 letter. Most people don't know what it means and they they're terrified. They rush in our office after receiving a letter from the IRS thinking that their paycheck will be garnished.

You can relax. The IRS is not out to get you, or put you in

"If we can't get you no money – it can't be got"

jail. We talk to the IRS all the time. For the most part, they're good people to work with. Occasionally, we get someone who doesn't enjoy their job, but that's very rare. Most of the time, they're very helpful. They're certainly not out finger pointing wrong doers. They have a job to do and simply want to make sure you're filing your taxes correctly and all the numbers add up correctly.

Audits are performed randomly and in the unlikely event you are audited, we'll stand behind you. We'll communicate with the IRS on your behalf. If you happened to have your taxes prepared by another tax office and audited by the IRS, that's fine. We'll stand behind you, and instruct you of the audit process.

Rest assured, there's usually a way we can solve your problem and eliminate worry.

The Fundamentals
of an IRS Audit

If you ever receive a letter from the IRS, make sure you respond in a timely manner. The worst possible thing you can do is not respond.

An audit is not necessarily saying you were wrong. The only thing an audit is saying is something didn't add up, or didn't look right. For example, the child you claimed may have already been claimed as a dependent by someone else and the IRS wants to ensure that that the rightful client claims the dependent.

"If we can't get you no money – it can't be got"

There are different types of audits. The most common audits are called Earned Income Tax Credit (EITC) audits. This audit affects your filing status such as Head of Household, Single, Married Filing Jointly, Married Filing Separate, or Widowed. This audit will also affect your itemized deductions. The IRS is only trying to get a clarification on these matters.

If you don't respond to the IRS, your tax return will be changed based upon their findings from the audit. At this point, you may challenge their findings with evidence you may have. If your evidence is not substantial the tax return remains in favor of the audit findings and is finalized. However, you do have the option to go to court and challenge the IRS findings.

A lot of people choose not to go to IRS court because they feel they'll automatically lose up against the IRS. Truth is, many times, the case doesn't go to court. It's resolved between you and an arbitrator. An arbitrator is a third party not associated with the IRS, or the person being audited that listens to the case and based on findings the case is settled unbiased.

More than likely, the person who prepares your audit may have taken a few classes, pass a 3-part exam, and became an Enrolled Agent, ultimately getting a job with the IRS.

A lot of people think if they do something wrong on their taxes, the IRS is going to knock on their door, slap a pair

"If we can't get you no money – it can't be got"

of handcuffs on them, and haul them off to jail. That's not true at all.

The IRS doesn't make phone calls. They only send letters. At some point, many of our clients have been scammed from receiving a call from someone claiming to be part of the IRS. They'll say you owe the IRS a certain amount of money or you will be prosecuted. These are scare tactics used by "scammers" who capitalize on fear and lack of knowledge of IRS procedures.

When we get involved, we stop these scammers right in their tracks. We let our clients know they're being "targeted" as part of a scam. Many of our clients have been led to believe they're going straight to jail. As a result, they pay what the scammer says is due. They then proceed to their bank and mail a cashier check to the scammers. This scam has affected many unsuspecting people.

Once again, the IRS doesn't call. They only send letters. If for some reason they do call, it's because you asked them to call you.

"If we can't get you no money – it can't be got"

Chapter 6

The Earned Income
Tax Credit
(EITC)

The Earned Income Credit was put in place to help the poor rise above the poverty line.

Years ago, the federal government realized that a large portion of the American population was living below the poverty line. For a larger percentage of people to live above the poverty line, our government had to create a program that would help these individuals rise above the poverty line. The EITC has helped families with a child (or children) to enjoy a higher quality of life by utilizing the credit.

The United States is deeply in debt. The more jobs created, allows for more withholdings. The federal government can collect the interest from our withholdings. This method assists in running the country and pays for infrastructures, roads, bridges, and public safety.

If you make a certain amount of money, the government doesn't necessarily penalize you. Instead, you are required to pay a higher percentage of taxes than someone who

"If we can't get you no money – it can't be got"

makes less money. The money is withheld for twelve months and at the end of that period the government returns the money and retains the interest from the withheld money. That's America's way of asking you, as a taxpayer, to contribute to society.

We cannot do away with our current tax system. Otherwise, there would be no way to pay for our military, our police departments, or any government agencies in America. I believe our tax system is the best thing the United States has.

Understanding
The Earned Income
Tax Credit

If a person is single without a child, and they have worked a job all year round, the first thing that comes to mind is "I'm going to owe money." They think to themselves, because I'm single, I'm going to have to pay. They don't realize that according to the wages they make, and the withholdings the government takes out of their check, they don't need to have a dependent to receive a return.

The Earned Tax Credit

The United States Federal Earned Income Tax Credit (EITC) is a refundable tax credit for low to moderate-income working individuals and couples. This credit is particularly helpful to people with children.

"If we can't get you no money – it can't be got"

The amount of EITC benefit depends on a recipient's income and number of children. For a person or couple to claim one or more persons as their qualifying child, requirements such as relationship, age, and residency must be met.

Many people have a misunderstanding about the EITC.

The Earned Tax Credit
Has Four Components:

- Single without child
- Single with one child
- Single with two children
- Single with three children

Many people believe that if they don't have a child they will not qualify for the EITC credit.

Humans don't look at our tax returns. Computers do everything. The IRS computer looks through millions and millions of names and W2's. In the process, it matches up huge amounts of information. When it spots something that doesn't make sense, it rejects the information. For example, Mr. Smith is single and earns $24,000 during the year and has a withholding of $1,600. Based on the given numbers, the IRS computer will say that Mr. Smith "owes" money.
Mr. Smith's taxes are filed as a single individual. The IRS computer doesn't take into consideration that Mr. Smith has deductions.

"If we can't get you no money – it can't be got"

There are many deductions Mr. Smith could take advantage of. To name a few, he may have deductions for tax preparation from a previous year tax return, deductions for medical and doctor expense, and for health insurance. The problem is the IRS computer system is not aware of the allowed deductions and base Mr. Smith's tax returns on the information at hand not including any deductions.

If you don't have a qualified tax preparer review your taxes, the IRS will assume you owe money. Since many people don't know what to do, they don't do anything, and end up paying. All it takes is one time for this to occur and you become hesitant.

Once someone has a negative experience with the IRS, they are viewed as "The Big Bad Wolf."

It's like having a toothache. If you don't fix it, the pain gets worse. The same is true with the IRS and your taxes. Your tax situation will not go away. If you don't file, things will only get worse. No matter your situation, it's always better to file, than to not do anything. That's never a good option.

Every year the IRS comes up with their formula for EITC (Earned Income Tax Credit). For instance, the guidelines may say if you have one child, you will be eligible to receive, let's say $3,200. These are not the actual numbers. I'm just providing an example as to how the system works. If this individual has a second child, they would be eligible

"If we can't get you no money – it can't be got"

to receive $4,800. If they have a third child, they would qualify for $5,400 EITC. Now, let's take that scenario a step further.

The EITC is popular with families and individuals. It's also the most misunderstood credit in the tax business. The guidelines can be confusing. In fact, an entire book could be written on this subject.

For example, let's assume we have a client who tells us he's worked all year, and has three children. He might assume he qualifies for the full $5.400 tax credit, but that's not necessarily true. It doesn't always work that way.

Let me explain. As of the printing of this book, the maximum amount of credit for the year 2016, (without a child) is $506. To clarify, this is for a single individual, with no children, and has worked all year.

Many of our customers don't understand this part of the EITC process. They fear they're going to owe taxes. They do not realize they can still qualify for the $506 in earned income credit.

A person with one child can get $3,373 for a child. If a person has two children, they can get $5,572; with three children, they can qualify for $6,269.

For the sake of this example, let's say you're head of household and make $14,000 with one child. Your federal withholding tax is $1,400 based on 10% of your total

income. You would be eligible for the $3,373. Keep in mind; you would have to make the full $14,000 to be eligible for the tax credit. If you make $39,296, you would not be eligible to receive the Earned Income Tax Credit.

Often during tax season, someone will walk in our office and tell us a tax preparer down the street told them they qualified for a big refund, plus the full EITC tax credit. We'll do a quick review of their paperwork, and realize right away they were given bad advice. We must tell them the bad news — that they don't qualify for a big refund and tax credit. When they hear our answer, as you might imagine, they're not happy. Some people walk out of our office and end up filing with the preparer who promised them a bigger return. The customer is happy, that is, until they get a letter from the IRS telling them they're being audited.

To make matters worse, most tax mistakes take a while to rear their ugly head. When someone eventually gets a letter from the IRS, guess what they do? They return to their originally tax preparer, only to find out the doors are locked and the lights are turned off. The company is either closed for the rest of the year — or worse — they've gone out of business.

That's when things deteriorate. These people have been victimized. They're left high and dry with nobody to help them. Eventually, many of these same individuals hear about our services, and that we're open all year round and come to us hoping we can solve their problems.

"If we can't get you no money – it can't be got"

We spend a lot of time fixing other tax preparers' mistakes. That's why we stay open all year round. During the offseason, we work closely with the IRS to correct tax filing issues created by other tax preparers. Many of these preparers close their offices for one reason or another.

Chapter 7

Head of Household

Head of household is a subject many people are misinformed about. Often people have children and they come into a tax office and say, "I have a dependent." A dependent is an individual that has resided with you for more than six months in your care. The taxpayer "assumes" they're the "head of the household," but that's not always the case.

To receive the "head of household" status on a tax return, you should be the one who pays the essential bills. Bills like electric… water… and rent. These are essential bills. Some people will tell us they pay the cable bill. That's not an essential bill. A cable bill is a "novelty" bill. Water, electricity, food and rent — these are essentials bills.

People also believe that head of household is going to get them more money. Being single, and head of household are very much the same.
The only difference is, single with a child is that, they don't pay any of the essential bills. They'll say "I stay there, but I'm not head of the household. Head of household means one thing and "single" means another. Head of household does not necessarily mean you get

"If we can't get you no money – it can't be got"

more money. It only gives the IRS the indicator of who is "head of household," who is single, and who stays at what address.

For instance, let's say Tim and Mary are a couple. We'll say they share the same household, but they're not married. The house is in Tim's name. He pays the electric and water bill. Tim is classified as "head of household." Mary will be classified as "single," if they file taxes separately, which in this example, they would do. Neither one of them could claim each other because neither one are dependent on each other, if they are not married or common-law.

Also, while we are talking about head of household, we should talk about married filing jointly and married filing separate.

If Mary and Tim were married, they would file jointly. Let's say their standard deductions are $12,400. That amount is deducted from their annual gross income (AGI). If they are married, but filing separate, they'll only receive $6,200 apiece. Let's say Mary and Tim filed jointly, and both went to Daytona State College. The IRS will give them a credit, called the American Opportunity Tax Credit. They both will receive up to a $1,000 each. In other words, Mary and Tim will get back up to $2,000 credit for going to school. Plus, whatever else they're going to get back for their withholdings, etc.

If they filed as married, but separate — even though both

went to school — neither one of them can receive that credit. When you are married, and file separate, the only thing the IRS allows you to claim is your deductions. If you have children involved, you will not be able to receive the Earned Income Tax Credit.

If a couple is married and files separately, they're not going to get anything. They may try to file as single, and get around IRS guidelines. This can backfire. My advice would be to collaborate and figure out what to do. At this point, neither one of them will get any money back.

When a couple is married, and files separate, they're required to put each other's Social Security numbers on their respective tax returns. When the IRS computer scans their information, it picks up these inconsistencies. It triggers a red flag. When this happens, the IRS orders an audit to figure out what's going on. The couple ends up getting audited, ultimately having to pay back the money owed. People faced with such situations often end up coming to us to help sort things out.

A lot of the bigger tax companies send new hires through a fast-paced tax course. In many cases, these courses are crammed into only a day or two. Its mind boggling to think these companies would try and train someone to be a qualified "tax preparer," after only a day or two of classes. That's impossible. It takes most tax preparer's years to understand the complexities of the IRS and our tax system.

New tax preparers are eager to find clients because they get paid based on the number of tax returns they can do.

"If we can't get you no money – it can't be got"

It's a numbers game.

Make no mistake about it, the more customers a tax preparer can shuffle through these big tax preparation companies the more money they make. Good for them, bad for you causing room for errors to occur.

Is that how you want to be treated? I doubt it.

The average person who comes to our office will spend at least 20 minutes with us. We don't rush people through the process. It's too important to them, and us. Money is at stake and the client's interest is our priority.

"If we can't get you no money – it can't be got"

Chapter 8

Self-Employment

Many people are misinformed about self-employment.

Many of our clients come into our office, and disclosed they're "self-employed." They don't understand that in the eyes of the IRS, it's quite serious to classify yourself as "self-employed."

Allow me to explain…

Even though it's written in the Publication 17, it says that anyone who makes over $400 a year should file a tax return. This is a publication the IRS has written. If you think about it, everybody is a part of society.

For example, if you are a thief or drug dealer, what do you put on your tax return? Why should someone who makes an income illegally, file a tax return, even if they're a drug dealer? These are some of the questions that haven't been answered by the IRS. I can't answer them either.

The IRS covers this information in their publications. It's important you understand when you file as "self-employed" you are at a much greater risk of being audited, than any other status.

"If we can't get you no money – it can't be got"

Let's say, for example, an individual has one child. Typically for one child, making over $6,400, the government will provide that person a $3,000 EIC credit. That is assuming the individual made $6,400 for that tax year.

To continue that thought, let's say a single mom comes to a tax preparer. She says she has one child. She also claims to own her own business as a hairdresser. She tells the preparer she's been doing hair out of her kitchen, but cannot provide any receipts. She also has no records of her day-to-day operation. She insists she her profession is a hairstylist. This individual's claim puts a tax preparer in a very difficult situation. The tax preparer can stay ethical, or do something unethical.

If that same individual came into our office, and did not have any records or receipts to prove their self-employed status, we would not do their taxes. Their situation, based on IRS guidelines, would be considered unethical.

Some tax preparers do not care that you don't have receipts or proper documents to support a self-employed status. If the customer says they made at least $6,400, and have one child, some tax preparers will do their taxes. Not only that, but they'll also tell the customer they can get a $4,300 return. This includes the additional credit for the Child Tax Credit, which qualifies for an additional $1,000, if the child is under the age of 17. So now, you have

"If we can't get you no money – it can't be got"

$3,700 for the EITC, and an additional $1,000 on top of that. This adjustment brings the potential for a total tax return of approximately $4,700.

That's a lot of money. It's very appealing to anyone claiming to be self-employed. But, it's wrong, and an ethical tax preparer would not file someone's taxes as self-employed status. But far too often, that's not what happens.

Many tax preparers will look at this scenario, and think to themselves, this person is getting a $4,870 tax return. Instead of telling the person they don't qualify for self-employed status, they allow them file as self-employed and they charge the client $1,000 to prepare their taxes. Essentially, they've taken a bad situation, and made it worse.

No tax return should be more than $750.00. And, if the fee is that high, it means the individual had a complicated tax return, with many deductions. It requires a lot of work by the tax preparer, justifying the higher fee.

In these situations, these tax preparers or "wolves," are charging people $700, $800, maybe even $1,000 more than they should. They're taking advantage of the client and neither party deserves the money they're claiming.

If a tax preparer has ten people come into their office, and charges each of them $1,000 — they just made $10,000. So, they're doing something just as unethical as the person

"If we can't get you no money – it can't be got"

who is claiming to be self-employed.

Meanwhile, the individual's tax return is "on the radar" at the IRS computer. On their form 1040, it shows the client reporting as self-employment status.

Weeks or months may pass. Eventually, an IRS computer will catch the individual's return, and a red flag will go up. A human being will review the returns, and realize something doesn't add up. The IRS representative will also notice the tax preparer charged the person $1,000 to prepare the individual's taxes. An IRS office decides to send out a letter and want the individual to prove she is self-employed. When the person can't prove what they've claimed, they'll end up having to pay the money back.

People must know when you are doing self-employment the first thing a business does is register with the IRS. It's called an Employment Identification Number (EIN). This indicates that you are a business entity.

The next step is the assignment of a bank account. Your bank account must be in the business name, not your individual name. This indicates your business not only has an EIN number, you also have a bank where receivables in which money comes in and goes out. This method establishes a paper trail.

For instance, let's say you cut and style hair from your home. You must show the IRS certain documents to support these claims. They'll want proof of what you say

"If we can't get you no money – it can't be got"

you've done, like specific dates for the appointments you had receipts for the fees you charged, and the services you provide.

If you are audited, you'll need the three things that show you are a true "self-employed" business. When you don't have those three things, the IRS considers this a "hobby," not a business. They'll see it something you do periodically, even though you might do it every day. The problem is, you don't have any records to support your claims as a business. You won't have a leg to stand on if you cannot prove you're a business.

Without proper records such as bank account and EIN number, you have nothing to support your claim. Without proper documentation, the IRS will consider what you do, a hobby.

The "self-employed" status misleads many people and being taken advantage of by unethical tax preparers and getting the IRS involved; makes matters much worse.

Filing as "self-employed" can raise many red flags. Never file as self-employed if you don't have the proper records and IRS requirements to support it because it could have serious consequences.

For example, if the IRS feels you haven't provided enough evidence to support your self-employed status, not only are you likely to subject yourself to an audit; you will also have to return the money to the IRS if you live in HUD

"If we can't get you no money – it can't be got"

housing (Housing & Urban Development), you could lose your status and possible evicted from your HUD housing.
.

If the IRS determines you are making earnings that haven't been reported, you could lose three ways.

1.) You could lose the $1,000.00 collected from you. There's a good chance the tax preparer won't be around to refund your money. So, you'll lose in that manner.

2.) You'll owe the money you received on your tax return due to not be able to prove your income or deductions.

3.) You will stand a good chance of possible eviction from your HUD housing

So, for $4,800 you received when you filed your taxes — you could potentially lose it all. Everything! Don't be tempted to do this. Sadly, we see it happen year after year.

Self-employment status is completed on the IRS form, "Schedule C". In the eyes of the IRS you can have a bank account even if money is not being deposited in the account.

In this instance, IRS pays very close attention to your filing status.

"If we can't get you no money – it can't be got"

Chapter 9

Education Credit

The Education Credit is very misunderstood. It's referred to as the American Opportunity TAX Credit, or the AOTC. The American Opportunity Tax Credit is for people who go to a "credited" college or trade school, after high school.

The AOTC was designed to give people who want to continue their education, an incentive to do so. It was put in place for the parent who wants to help their child with continued education.

In most cases, a parent will claim the tax on their tax return, because the child is still a dependent. This applies even though the child may be going to college or trade school.

Just because you don't claim the individual on your tax return, doesn't mean you can't get a tax break on your taxes. The AOTC is a "credit" for helping.

For example, a grandparent may help pay for their grandchild's books, housing. They would still qualify for a percentage of the AOTC even though the child is a dependent of their parent. That's because Grandma and

Grandpa also contributed as well.

Many people are under the impression that only one person can make this claim a child's education expenses. This is not true. These days, it can take an entire family to send a child to college or trade school.

At what point do you decide who gets the credit? According to the laws governing education, both parties can receive money for their part in their child's (or grandchild's) education.

"If we can't get you no money – it can't be got"

Chapter 10

Itemized Deductions

Many people come into our tax office that makes an adequate income. They're worried because they may make, say $100,000 a year, but don't have any dependents. They think they're going to owe the IRS a lot of money. As a result, they seek our advice.

A lot of unqualified tax preparers don't understand that itemized deductions are the most important factor in these type situations. Most are unaware of the guidelines for "itemized deductions." They don't have the knowledge of what can and cannot be considered a "deduction."

Many preparers could use a whole month reading about deductions. For instance, if you were part of an investment group or club, and your club sold some stocks (securities), you can deduct your share of expenses. You'd be surprised how many tax preparers don't know this. This deduction applies to whatever your expenses were in your club, at the time you sold your shares. This is true whether you profited or lost money. The IRS allows you to deduct your expenses from that experience.

"If we can't get you no money – it can't be got"

Medical Deductions

Many people don't know that if they take their parent to the doctor's office, they can deduct the mileage from their house to the doctor's office and back to their house. That's called a Medical Mileage Deduction.

An individual can also deduct the co-pay on their insurance. Let's say your doctor prescribes an inhaler for a respiratory infection. For example, the inhaler costs you $200; this medical expense is deductible. Also, any prescribed medication you have is deductible. Many tax preparers and taxpayers do not have knowledge of this.

The amount that is deducted is considered two percent of your adjusted gross income (AGI.) So, if you made $100,000, two percent of that figure is $2,000. Anything after $2,000, entitles you to the itemized deduction.

Every time you pay your medical premium, after that accumulates after your Adjusted Gross Income (AGI), it becomes deductible.

Visiting a hospital emergency room and having to wait several hours, you decide to purchase something to eat your meal cost is deductible. If you happen to have a need to purchase crutches, that expense is also deductible. Having a safe deposit box is also deductible. Working from home also allows a portion of your utility expenses to also be deductible. A home office allows for a huge deduction.

"If we can't get you no money – it can't be got"

Knowing even a little bit about your deductions can be a big help to you. We see the opposite of that all the time. People come in not having a clue about their tax rights. They'll walk in, thinking they're they owe the IRS a large sum of money. When we do their taxes, and tell them they only owe $3,000. They'll look at us and say, "Are you kidding? What did you do?

Many people put us on a pedestal all the time, making us out to be superheroes. We're not we just take our jobs seriously.

If you make approximately $100,000 a year, chances are you're in some sort of professional field. At some point, you probably do some level of work at home. That's called "the business use of home." It's a huge deduction and often overlooked by a lot of tax preparers.

I have an office set up in my home. That's not all. I also have a desk, computers, and printers in my home office. I work from home a great deal. It's part of my job and it's all tax deductible.

Itemized deductions are something a tax preparer must understand backwards and forwards and should be second nature. Otherwise, critical deductions are overlooked that you might otherwise qualify for. If you get a feeling your tax preparer has not "mastered" self-employed tax deductions; I recommend you pick up your paperwork and go somewhere else. Trust your gut feeling if you don't think someone is qualified or legitimate and keep searching.

You'll quickly discover when you ask many "so called" tax preparers questions about self-employed tax deductions that many will stumble and stammer with their responses. If that happens, I suggest that you look elsewhere for a qualified tax preparer and not a wolf in sheep's clothing.

Chapter 11

Conclusion

Responsibilities of Being a Tax Preparer

Tax Preparers have a very important job. Most important is gaining the trust of the client. Establishing a positive relationship occurs in the initial interviewing process. It is quite essential to ask the appropriate questions that are relevant to the client so that a proper tax return can be prepared. Examining taxes from the prior year is also a good strategy as well.

Collecting and discussing the client's financial matters can be such an invasive and personal situation. However, the process of collecting income statements, W-2's, itemized expense documents, receipts, date of births, and Social Security numbers is part of the process to complete a return.

As a tax preparer, our responsibility is to ensure that you do not pay unnecessary taxes, resolve tax questions, and recommend additional products to improve your financial status.

You and your finances are what matters to us.

"If we can't get you no money – it can't be got"

Establishing an ethical culture at Farrell Tax and Services is a priority. Our values match our actions. We can achieve this level of ethical behavior by allowing transparency. The number one question my partner or myself will ask before any work is performed is, does the decision feel like the right thing to do?

Sounds so simply. Right? However, many tax preparers cannot master this simple question and answer with sureness.

Farrell Tax and Services take an active responsibility making sure that are actions are consistent and our principles can be defended publicly. As part of this process, levels of continuing education in tax preparation is a necessity.

Tax rules and issues constantly change and as an established tax office, our access to information should always remain current to give the best tax advice to our clients.

As a tax client, you have rights and obligations to secure your financial future. Tax preparation is a huge integral portion of the process as well as other financial range of services that require specializations and planning.

We want our clients to be informed and feel assured that our expertise proves beneficial and always with accuracy.

"If we can't get you no money – it can't be got"

In preparation of writing **The IRS Is NOT the 'Big Bad Wolf,** we wanted to ensure that accurate and current information was relayed to better prepare you as tax clients. One of our goals is to educate the public to avoid falling prey to unethical tax preparers. We understand that it is a frustrating process to prepare your taxes. However, with the information provided, we feel that some of those frustrations are eliminated and replaced with confidence.

I have spent countless hours contemplating the process of how to have such relevant information available to the public.

I can proudly say that throughout my years as a professional tax preparer that the ethical treatment of our clients is of most importance. At Farrell Tax and Services, we work as a team to get the job done.

"If we can't get you no money – it can't be got"

For more information on how we can help you with your taxes go to www.IRSandMe.com or call our office at: (386) 333-9293.

<u>Disclaimer</u>

The information in this book should not be used in any transaction without the advice and guidance of a tax preparer that is familiar with all the relevant facts.
<u>The examples in this book are not actual numbers or accounts.</u>

Furthermore, the information contained herein may not be applicable to or suitable for the individuals' specific circumstances or needs and may require consideration of other matters.

While we have made every attempt to ensure that the information contained in this book has been obtained from reliable sources, Farrell Tax and Services is not responsible for any errors or omissions, or for the results obtained from the use of this information.

"If we can't get you no money – it can't be got"